THE UNCOMMUNIST MANIFESTO

ALEKS SVETSKI
AND MARK MOSS

Contents

Acknowledgments

This book would not have been possible without the blend of standing on the shoulders of giants, the madness going on in the world today, and the support of our patrons on KickStarter; John Galt, P.Mileman, @gauchoeddy, Mark E. Jeftovic, The Joseph Family, The Vine Yard, James H Frederick IV, Greg Mantz, Barra, Francisco Tomé Costa, Robin Choong, Scott Brehaut, Gordon Christian and The Digital Playhouse in Agnes Water.

We'd like to thank you all, alongside thinkers such as Murray Rothbard, Ludwig von Mises, Friedrich A Hayek, and Hans Herman Hoppe for the work they've done this past century in illuminating human action, Austrian economics and the sound principles upon which the dynamic nature of the world can be understood.

We'd like to thank Satoshi Nakamoto for Bitcoin. Arguably the most important invention, or discovery, not just this century, but as Aleks would argue, "since cavemen discovered fire".

We'd like to thank the founding fathers of America for their strength and courage in breaking away from the tyranny of a broken, dysfunctional hierarchy and giving us a place where the freedom to express oneself still exists (albeit the recent erosion).

We want to thank the clown world simulation of the recent years for helping challenge us, forcing us to grow and become better versions of ourselves. Every stupidity has a silver lining and if this is part of the learning process or the price humanity must pay to transform into a more moral, just and functional world, then so be it. While modernity may have induced many into psychosis or ignorance, it has also awakened millions and caused them to search within on their pursuit of truth.

We want to thank (sort of) Marx and Engels, for writing the original piece. We disagree with almost everything you said and wrote, but at least you made us aware of how society can devolve into the worst version of itself if it succumbs to entropy of the mind and spirit. Your legacy will be such that you inspired the counter force, and the rise of the Sovereign Individual.

And lastly, we'd like to thank all of you, for taking the time to read this book. May it inspire your soul to reach for the stars.

Preface

The UnCommunist Manifesto is an answer, or perhaps antidote to the nihilism, despair, and chaos individuals are facing in the modern world.

Counter-inspired by the infamous "Communist Manifesto" by Marx & Engels, this short book hopes to challenge what may be unconsciously acquired biases and beliefs people of all walks of life are carrying with them.

As such, instead of just diving into the manifesto, we took the time out to write a unique glossary of terms, which at first glance you might think are unrelated, but as the 4 chapters proceeding it unfold, will come to make sense.

In this book, we hope to dispel the idea that individuals can be arbitrarily classified into groups and judged as such. We argue that people are neither their race, nor their work, their nationality, politics, color, creed or economic status.

They are individuals. Characterized by their own beliefs, values and virtues, who can only be judged by the behavior displayed through their individual, independent action.

Our goal was to reorient the axis away from some fantastical political spectrum in which the struggle between oppressor and oppressed is all that matters, and toward a more tangible, realistic struggle; the journey to becoming a sovereign individual, of claiming one's autonomy and of the struggle necessary to become the best version of yourself.

The axis of the real struggle of life is not one arbitrarily defined class versus another.

It is the individual whose spirit wants to reach, versus the collective; whose constant desire it is to transform humans into automatons and thus extinguish the spirit.

Our other goal was to redefine the political spectrum and separate it out from the organic, natural processes of innovation, evolution and what we've termed 'natural capitalism'. This element will indeed challenge many preconceived notions and we believe much of the value of this book will come from this alone.

Our final hope is that this book too will be read far and wide over the coming centuries as the world evolves at a far greater pace. It will be interesting to see whether The Communist or UnCommunist Manifesto truly stands the test of time.

Thank you for taking the time to read this and to challenge yourself.

Aleks Svetski & Mark Moss

May 2022

Definitions

The importance of clearly defining terms at the outset cannot be overstated.

In order for us to speak the same language, and come to some form of understanding, we must agree on what specific words mean.

The following, rather unconventional, glossary will lay the groundwork for this, after which the assertions and position of the book will make sense.

A Priori

Knowledge considered true in the absence of experience or observation. Knowledge that requires no evidence. Like 1+1 = 2. It does not need a series of experiments to prove it. A priori comes from Latin "from the previous" or "from the one before."

A Posteriori

Knowledge learned from experience and observation. It involves evidence. It is the opposite of a priori knowledge. A Latin phrase meaning "from the latter"

Adaptability

Similar to fitness, it is the ability and willingness to change in order to suit different conditions. It is critical in order to survive and thrive in a constantly changing environment.

Bourgeoisie

The term used by Marx to arbitrarily classify the group of individuals with property. They were middle to upper class and generally the entrepreneurs, business owners and industrialists.

Bitcoin

Perfect, fixed supply money and an open, borderless, permissionless network. Its decentralized nature makes it censorship resistant and it enables anybody anywhere to securely move value anywhere in the world, at any time, without an administrator or authority.

Cantillon Effect

Named after the 18th century economist Richard Cantillon, it explains that the arbitrary creation of new money in the absence of new goods will result in not just more money chasing the same number of goods, therefore causing the average price to rise (inflation), but because it takes time for this new money to filter into the economy, price inflation does not occur simultaneously with monetary inflation and results in a direct benefit to those closest to the money supply, at the detriment of those furthest from it.

Capital

Time, energy, matter / material resources, and their higher order products.

Capital extends to both the physical and metaphysical realm. Your thoughts are your most precious metaphysical form of capital, your time is your most scarce form of objectively measurable capital, and natural resources are a form of scarce physical, tangible capital.

Capitalism

Perhaps the most misunderstood of all the words in this list. Capitalism is simply another word for progress, innovation or evolution.

Capitalism is not a system of rule, rules or politics.

It is an organic process that happens in all living or complex systems.

It is inherently apolitical.

No 'body' is in 'charge' of it, nor can there be 'forms' of political capitalism. Capitalism just 'is'.

When we subtract all of the political definitions projected on it, we find that it is simply the natural process of taking resources (time, energy, matter) and turning them into something of higher order, quality or value.

All systems of rule, order and organization, even socialism and communism, have capitalism "in" them. The question is simply; to what degree is this natural process allowed to occur, and to what degree does politics and the short-sighted human desire to control everything get in the way?

Capitalism's forcing functions are efficiency and effectiveness, its corrective mechanism is loss, and its positive feedback loop is growth.

If an economy is a complex system made up of human interactions, capitalism is the word we give to its evolutionary process.

Central Planning

The concentration or centralization of research, analysis, planning and decision making. This model of operation is a distinguishing feature of modern governments, policy groups and of course, central bankers.

In some contexts, it allows for faster decision making, but it does not scale because planning for another implies knowing what they want or need in that particular moment. This is impossible in complex systems such as human societies or economies because the quantity of information available and processing power required to analyze, let alone decide on everything, is incalculable. As such this mode of planning fails as it scales.

Competition

The forcing function of evolution. The reality of a world in which resources are unevenly distributed, time is unidirectional and energy is scarce. Complex systems and living organisms must strive to survive. As such, rivalries between entities (whether cells, multicellular organisms, individuals, businesses or social groups) emerge as they vie for the scarce resources necessary for their survival.

This process is the forcing function of adaptability and fitness, which are the central themes of evolution.

Communism

Karl Marx himself told us that *"the theory of the Communists may be summed up in the single sentence: Abolition of private property."*

Complex Systems

A complex system is one that is composed of many pieces all interrelated and interacting with each other. Examples of complex systems include: the human body, the earth's macro and micro climates, the economy, the internet, Bitcoin, etc.

Complex systems are difficult (if not impossible) to model

due to dependencies, competition, relationships and myriad other unknown interactions between their parts or between the given system and its environment.

Correction

A modifying behavior all complex systems exhibit when they are no longer in equilibrium. Corrections occur as a result of feedback mechanisms signaling over-extension, distortion or, in some cases, impact or influence by external stimuli. This is a perfectly natural, and critical process inherent to all living (complex) systems. Unfortunately, linear-minded people seem to think this is somehow a problem.

Deflation

Deflation, as the name implies, is the opposite of inflation. It generally refers to a contraction in quantity or a diminishing supply of that which is being measured. In an economic sense, it is often (incorrectly) used to signify a contracting market, but in Austrian economics, deflation refers to 'price deflation'. This is desirable because it is inline with the natural progression of innovation. In other words, the better we get at things, the cheaper they should become because we can do more with less. This is also inline with the forcing functions of evolution and natural capitalism, ie; efficiency and efficacy.

Decentralization

The distribution of analysis, decision making and action to the edges of a system. A process by which the activities of an organization, particularly those regarding planning and decision making, are distributed or delegated away from a central, authoritative location or group.
The opposite of centralization.

Diversity

The state of having many different, distinct and even divergent forms of types, ideas, or any particular thing. Note that equality is the natural opposite of diversity. Diversity requires variation, difference, nuance and degrees. Diversity is what enables life and results from the explore / experiment component of the evolutionary process.

Dystopia

A description of a future world or place in cataclysmic decline, where fear and distress run rampant under tyrannical governments.

They are unfortunately the necessary outcome of the pursuit of Utopian ideals. One person's Utopia is another's Dystopia, as such, neither are desirable.

Economics

Is the complex, non-empirical study of human action and the associated allocation of scarce resources, time and energy toward ends, bound by the constraints of physical reality.

Economics is the most basic study, and its integral analysis of incentive mechanisms can help us better understand everything from human psychology to biology, anthropology and even physics.

Economics is not math, nor science. It is more a 'meta', a 'way', a philosophy or a 'golden thread'. It is a set of principles through which value judgments can be made or understood.

Economics (Keyensian)

The attempt to reduce the irreducible study of economics into a set of models and mathematical formulas. All such economics is devoid of any relationship to the real world, because unlike empirical studies, human action and the complex nature of the world cannot be repeated in order to build a representative mathematical model. In other words, we cannot turn back time, life is not a game we can run on repeat and as such, modeling can at best tell us something about the past and little about the future.

Unfortunately, in today's day and age, it has become the means by which we make all grand economic decisions, via committee, resulting in the destruction of the precious human and natural capital we have at our disposal.

Emergence

The development of behaviors or properties within complex systems resulting from the interconnection, interrelation and interaction of the parts in the wider system, and not just a singular stimulus or isolated component.

Entropy

A metaphysical and measurably physical property of the universe most commonly associated with a progression away from order, and toward

chaos, disorder, randomness, or uncertainty.
Physically it's the loss of heat in a cup. Metaphysically it flows in the opposite direction of life.

Evolution

Evolution is what happens when organisms of any kind strive and compete for the scarce resources and energy needed to survive. The evolutionary result is greater fitness and adaptability. In biological systems this may mean a change in heritable characteristics over successive generations, and in an economy, it is the upward, progressive march of capitalism where better goods and services are produced with the use of less time, energy and resources.

Fair

When the rules of a game or system apply to every participant or entity. Fairness often gets confused with equality, but in truth, actually leads to inequality and diversity, both of which are desirable. A fair game will allow diverse participation because competition occurs across multiple dimensions. The key is that the agreed rules are the same. Think about a game of basketball (rules apply to all) and the diverse players (each player is different).
Equality is everybody getting the same thing regardless of their input or relative value. Fairness is everybody having the opportunity to get results commensurate to the relative quality or value of their inputs.

Feedback

A system's output. The information resulting from inputs. In a feedback loop, outputs of a system are routed back as inputs as part of a cause-and-effect chain.

Fiat

A decree, sanction, order, or top down pronouncement by a person or group of persons. The opposite of emergent and bottom up. Fiat or decrees by those who have absolute authority to enforce it are generally not aligned with natural order, emergent processes or observable reality. For example, Central Bank issued currencies have no value other than what is decreed by them and their counterparts in government.

Fitness

That which fits. The most adaptable, compatible and appropriate expression or instance of an entity. Competition is its forcing function.

Forcing Function

Is a behavior-shaping constraint or any task, activity or event that forces one to take action and produce a result.

In any system, the forcing function is an aspect of the design that prevents a user from taking an action without consciously considering information relevant to that action. In other words, it forces conscious attention upon something ("bringing consciousness to") and thus makes 'deliberate' or guides the performance of a task.

Freedom

The capacity to choose in the absence of coercion

Free Trade

When two or more individuals voluntarily exchange goods or services, once again in the absence of coercion, whether in the form of tarifs, taxes, or other racketeering, extortion, rent seeking and value extraction.

Free Market

A market or group of individuals engaging in the voluntary exchange of goods and services. The free market allows for price discovery and coordination of producers and consumers

Hierarchy

How systems organize, prioritize and select. A hierarchy is the structure that inevitably emerges when one must measure relative value, status, authority or competence in order to make a selection. Like all tools, it is apolitical and agnostic. It can be used to enable prioritization, focus and preference; or it can be used by fiat to suppress, oppress and exploit.

Information

Intelligent, coherent or some form of structured data, knowledge, physical or metaphysical material that can be transmitted, communicated, sent or received.

Incentive

Something that either induces action or motivates the application of effort. Encouragement via the hope of a reward or its counter, the fear of punishment. The promise of pleasure.

Individuality

The particular character or aggregate of qualities of a person or thing that distinguishes them from others of the same kind.

Inflation

Another poorly defined term because it depends on the context of what is being inflated. The core meaning of the word is the general increase in supply, volume or quantity of something. People generally refer to monetary inflation as defined below, but many other things can be inflated, from balloons (with air), to egos, to the volume of food on one's plate, the number of people born, the figures on a balance sheet and the powers given to a government.

Inflation (monetary)

Refers to the money supply and total number of a unit of account being used or issued. All forms of money since the dawn of time have been subject to inflation.
From promises to salt, to rocks, shells, metals and, in modern times, paper money and the digital numbers created on bank and central bank ledgers. Even gold is subject to inflation based upon how much can and is mined (albeit the inflation rate is low, see stock to flow). Bitcoin's supply inflates up to a predetermined maxima of 21,000,000, and is thus the first substance other than time or energy that is fixed in supply. The easier a money is to inflate, the easier it is to manipulate at the expense of another, the less accurately it can encode or represent non-inflatable time/energy, and the weaker its ability or guarantee to represent the product of one's labor. Inflatable money is a distorted, low fidelity and, therefore, a nonsensical language of value.

Independence

The product of freedom and responsibility.

Luddite

The Luddites were a secret oath-based organization of English textile workers in the 19th century, a radical faction which destroyed textile machinery. The group are believed to have taken their name from Ned Ludd, a weaver from Anstey, near Leicester, and, much like Marxists, had a low opinion of the progressive nature of innovation, competition and automation. They chose to destroy, not to build.

Market

An environment which facilitates the exchange of goods and services between buyers and sellers. When the exchange is done voluntarily, in the absence of a racketeer or other form of extortion (eg; taxation) it is known as a Free Market.

Money

The language of value.

Monopoly

A monopoly is a dominant, singular entity and sole provider of a good or service. A government is an example of such an entity, which holds a monopoly on the use of violence, the issuance of money and the creation of laws by decree.
Monopolies operate in a vacuum of competition and are not subject to market feedback, therefore they have no incentive to deliver a better product or service, at a better price. In other words, they lack the forcing functions of efficacy and efficiency found in an organic capitalist environment.

Moral Hazard

The act of taking risk, then placing the cost of any consequences on another party. In politics and government this is known as socializing losses. When you know someone or some other entity will pay for any resultant damage, your incentive to both take and hide risks increases.
It's a function of the risk taker having no "skin in the game."

Organic

Organic refers to a system of growth that is both natural and emergent. This growth usually occurs from within the bounds of the complex system.

Objective

That which is commonly or absolutely true. It is often contrasted with subjective, as if it's the opposite, but it is really the emergent property of a common subjective truth or observation. It also means, related to the above, to view or observe without bias or influence from an individual's personal (or subjective) viewpoint.

Parasite

An organism that lives and feeds on or in an organism of a different species and causes harm to its host. The parasite takes advantage of the value, energy or output of others without making any useful return.

Power

The amount of energy transferred or converted per unit time. In a social sense, it is the capacity to transmit energy or force, at scale, across time and can be done cooperatively or coercively.

Praxeology

Praxeology is the study of human action. It is a comprehensive discipline that takes into account the formal relationship between both human means and ends.

Praxeology contends we can not draw a clear line between economic actions and other types of goal-directed behavior. Because "choosing determines all human decisions," we must base our analysis of economic activity on a "general theory of choice and preference."

Proletariat:

As defined by Marx, a member of 'the working class' whose only possession is their labor.

Property:

Typically considered something tangible; land, goods, assets, etc, property extends to that which is both personal and intangible things such as: your own personal body, your thoughts, creativity and intellectual capital.

Private Property

The cornerstone of civilization, and the property explicitly owned by an individual or other private entity.

Public Property

Property that is not owned by an individual or private entity. Common or communal property. Subject to the tragedy of the commons.

Prices

Information in a market. The preferences and intersubjective valuations in a market place are transmitted in the form of prices. Prices are how we determine supply, demand, needs and wants and are part of the feedback mechanism inherent to a natural, organic market.

Prices are the signaling mechanism that enable coordination, value judgement and decision making on the part of market participants.

Responsibility

The corollary to freedom and the ability for an individual to self-impose restrictions aligned with some future-oriented desire, or that which is right or moral.

Socialism

A theory of social organization which advocates that the means of production, distribution, and exchange should be owned or regulated by the community as a whole. Unfortunately, decision making does not scale, so like other collectivist systems, falls victim to the dictates and decrees of the most politically adept representatives.

Stock to flow

Stock-to-flow ratios are used to evaluate the current stock of a commodity or good (total amount currently available) against the inflation or flow of new production (amount mined that specific year). The higher the Stock to Flow of a commodity or good, the more difficult it is to inflate, and thus the 'harder' it is.
Commodities such as gold, platinum, silver and substances such as bitcoin display a very high stock to flow ratio and are therefore used as stores of value across time.

Subjectivity

Individual perception. The absence of a common, objective standard. The variation in viewpoints, beliefs, ideas, conceptualization and value.

Time Preference

Also known as delayed gratification, time preference is the current relative value placed on receiving something in the present, compared to receiving it at a later date. Time preferences are represented mathematically as the 'discount' function, or Present Value / Future Value.
The 'certain present' will always be valued more than the 'uncertain future', so the ratio is always more than 1. The greater the value one places on the future (farsightedness, long term planning), the lower the time preference (and closer to 1). The opposite is also true.
Someone with a "low" time preference is willing to wait,

and practice delayed gratification, whereas someone with a "high" time preference would rather get something now, the future be damned. High time preference often results in wastage, and is a function of future uncertainty. Sound money and savings are forces that counteract this.

The selfish gene

In 1976 Richard Dawkins laid out a theory of survival through a gene-centered view of evolution. It gave us a biological basis for self-preservation and broadened our understanding of fitness, human behaviour and altruism. It is why in an Airplane emergency, you put your own mask on first, before assisting others.

The State

Murray Rothbard defines it as "*that organization in society which attempts to maintain a monopoly of the use of force and violence in a given territorial area; in particular, it is the only organization in society that obtains its revenue not by voluntary contribution or payment for services rendered but by coercion.*"

Utopia

An imaginary community or society that possesses highly desirable or nearly perfect qualities for its members. It was coined by Sir Thomas More for his 1516 book Utopia, describing a fictional island society in the New World.
We find it important to note that there is and never will be a 'Utopia for all' because individuals are diverse and one person's perfect, utopian vision could be another's dystopia.

Value

Value is the subjective preference assigned to an asset, good or service by an individual. Because all individuals vary in their wants, needs and desires, not only in relation or contrast to each other, but in relation and contrast to themselves at different times, in different contexts, value is subjective.
This brings with it the problem of intersubjectivity, which can only be solved with a common medium or language. In the case of value, we call this language or technology; 'money'.

Violence

The use or expression of intense force or great power, either as a natural phenomena (the storm was violent) or an action that is intended to harm and or kill someone or something.

Voluntary

The act of doing something of one's own volition, free from coercion. An individual is free when their choices are voluntary.

Chapter 1:
Static VS Dynamic Classes

The history of all hitherto existing society is the history of struggle, adaptation, innovation and creative destruction.

Whilst this has on occasion devolved into struggles of caste and class, those are merely one dimension of a much broader tapestry of 'struggle'.

All men and women, whether freeman, slave, artisan or manager, entrepreneur, artist, patrician, Christian, Muslim, shaman, monk, Asian, European, American, plebeian, lord, serf, guild-master, king, noble, warrior, general or soldier have at some stage stood in opposition to each other, *and* side by side with one another.

The dynamic emergence of human tribes, cultures and collectives in which competing & complementary models or philosophies have fought it out to discover how to best contend with the reality of lack, in an oftentimes harsh world, leaves individuals always with the choice to either cooperate, compete or oppress.

History, therefore, tells the story of humanity's two choices in dealing with each other and acquiring wealth. As Franz Oppenheimer put it; via either the economic or the political means.

1. The economic means involves the production and exchange of private property, goods and services by private individuals. This is the multiplicative method of voluntary exchange.

2. The political means is the simpler method of acquiring goods and services by the use of force, violence or coercion. This is the subtractive, zero sum method of one-sided confiscation.

The reality of this choice results in a world always in flux, swinging between the extremes of organic, emergent, individual freedom on one side, and top down, collective compulsion on the other.

Individual freedom is organized in a distributed fashion, across a multitude of dimensions and hierarchies of competence, whilst collective compulsion is organized in a centralized fashion by decree, which lead not to functional hierarchies, but to bloated, wasteful, morally repugnant bureaucracies.

If therefore the struggle of ours and all preceding ages can be summed up, it would be the individual fighting to maintain autonomy and independence, from the collective using political power to group individuals into classes in order to extract wealth. Of decentralization vs centralization. Of bottom up vs top down. Of natural and organic vs fiat and artificial.

Social Mobility

Perhaps the most pernicious of problems to plague humanity, in a social sense at least, is the ossification of classes. Whilst Marx may have been right to point out oppression between them, his error was to assume that there were only two classes, and that it was possible to somehow compress everybody into 'one class'.

As we've seen, this not only failed, because humans are diverse, but turned out to create two classes 'by decree', ie; the 'public representatives' who became "the state", amass all of the power and are above reproach, and the private individuals, who become slaves to the state.

The result is worse than feudalism, crony capitalism or caste systems. In fact, it leaves us with an even more stale caste-like system.

Marx and Engels point out:

> *"the modern bourgeois society that has sprouted from the ruins of feudal society has not done away with class antagonisms. It has but established new classes, new conditions of oppression, new forms of struggle in place of the old ones."*

Arbitrary class categorizations aside, this is of course true and is part of the dynamic nature of humanity's struggle throughout history. Their error was to assume society could come to some sort of end state converging on two classes, defined not by their constituent individuals but by the decree of Marx and Engels themselves.

They then assumed the answer was to 'do away' with one of the classes, and the final, working class would reach a point in which no struggle would exist. They were not only ignorant of human nature, but blind to the truth that life is but a journey of discovery and the endurance of a higher quality of struggle. To find the golden thread passing through each discipline, and use the principles one gleans to understand how best to live. This process is one of mobility. One in which you rise up and fall back down as a result of the consequences of your actions. The outcomes are unequally distributed, sure, but they are fair in a system where the rules apply to all.

Inequality is not a problem when you have social mobility. In fact, it's desirable, because it not only makes the world diverse, but gives individuals a meaningful future to strive for.

What Marx and other sterile, empirically-minded philosophers failed to realize is that humans are not driven primarily by the will to power, but by the will to meaning. Meaning requires something to strive toward and is something each individual must discover for themselves.

Furthermore, whilst many wish for more wealth, more assets and more property, others want the exact opposite. They would rather live free from material constraints and the responsibilities that weigh them down. Another example of the lack of understanding of human psychology on display in Marxist doctrine.

We therefore can organize society by some top down decree to limit power (which always fails because the top is where both the decrees come from and where the power concentrates), or we can allow it to emerge bottom up where individuals can discover their own meaning and strive to become the best versions of themselves.

History is littered with variations on hierarchies, and the common theme to date has been some sort of social mobility within largely static classes that have ossified over time through the replacement of competence with fiat or decree.

→ **Feudal: Hereditary fixed**

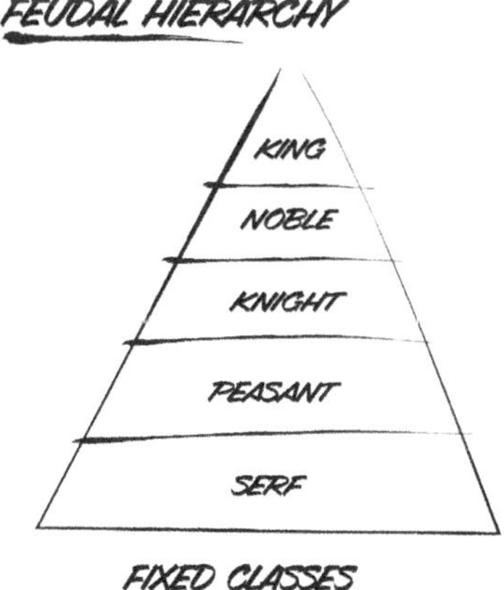

→ **Crony: Politically & Economically Fixed**

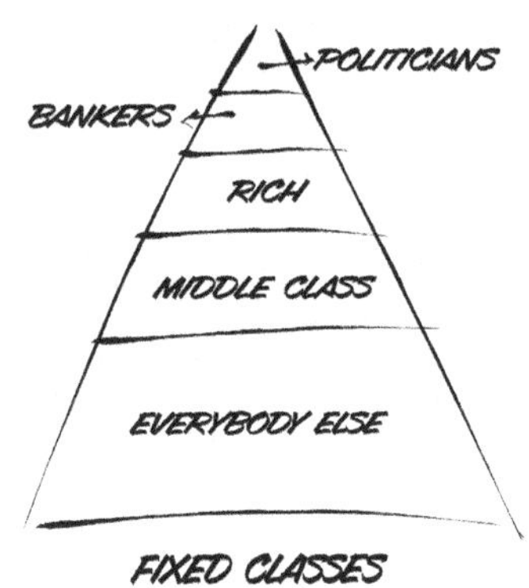

→ **Communist: Politically fixed**

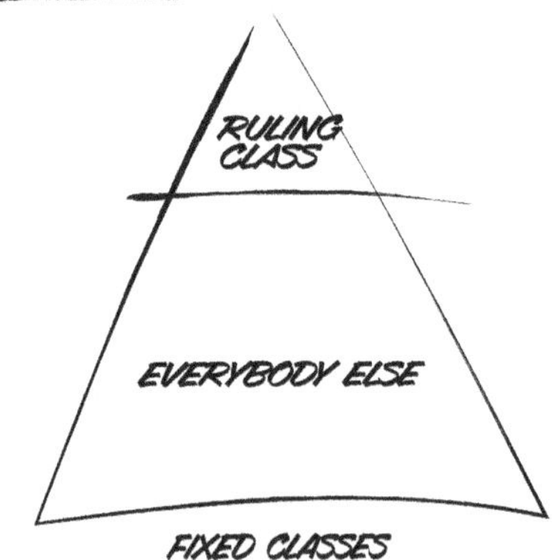

We propose a transformation and reorganization of society not by decree, but by the natural, emergent force of competence and liberty.

One of dynamic inequality, where classes continue to exist (they always will), but are permeable. Where the opportunity to rise up is available to all, and so too is everyone subject to the risk of failure and falling down the hierarchy. Upward motion becomes a function of work, competence, skill, talent, perseverance, desire, will and of course, luck. Downward motion a function of waste, poor calculation, mistakes, bad judgement, immoral behaviour, incompetence, laziness and of course, bad luck.

How can we do this?

Step one is *get out of the way.*

In doing so, individuals can take charge of their own future and become responsible, sovereign, competent versions of themselves in the dimensions they choose or are naturally predisposed toward.

Over time, it may look something like the below:

→ **Free market: Dynamic, social mobility**

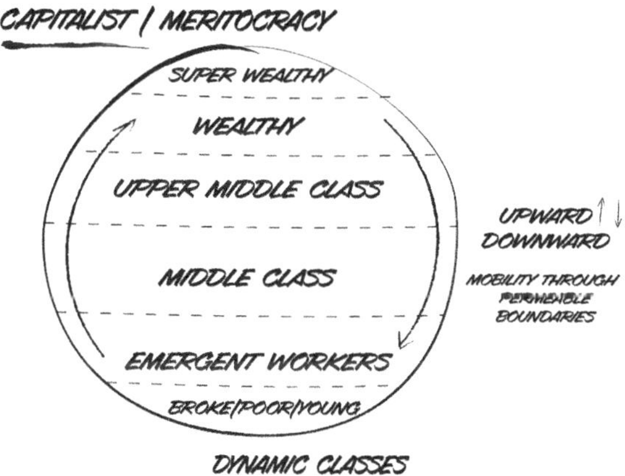

> *"the feudal relations of property became no longer compatible with the already developed productive forces; they became so many fetters. They had to be burst asunder; they were burst asunder."*

- Marx & Engels; The Communist Manifesto

Feudal hierarchies came face to face with hierarchies of competence and the result was natural, organic, free market forces transformed the prior feudal relations of property.

This was by definition an emancipating force for all those useful people under the thumb of largely stale, hereditary, feudal hierarchies.

Those hierarchies had emerged over the centuries, initially as a result of conquest, competence, bravery, valor and chivalry, but decayed through generations of rule by the entitled, cushioned, meaningless and the often-useless.

The so-called bourgeois class rose up and through the application of math, finance, science and technology were able to bring prosperity to millions and outcompete their prior overlords.

They provided more value, and the market chose. Evolution chose.

The problem occurred when the political parasites began to try and channel that natural force of collective human nature, (progress and innovation) and use it for political advantage.

To this degree, one could sympathize with Marx. A new group of political parasites replaced the old and were no better than the ones they had dethroned. Instead of honoring the process that enabled their emancipation, the nouveau riche created a new bureaucratic leviathan and formed regulatory moats that stifled not only progress but the opportunity for competent individuals to rise up themselves.

Dynamic Inequality

> *"Nobody is equal to anybody. Even the same man is not equal to himself on different days."*
>
> - Thomas Sowell

You cannot create dynamic equality by attempting to (however in vain) raise the level of those at the bottom. Rather, the system must allow for (as Taleb's ghost writer would say) the rich to rotate. In the context of status, in order for those at the 'bottom' to have the *possibility* to climb, the *possibility* to fall must exist for those at the top. And for it to remain organic and dynamic, neither can happen by force, but purely through competence or lack thereof.

The question is therefore **not**:

"How do we stop the motor of the world and create one static class ruled by one static public representative body?"

The question is:

"How do we ensure social mobility and a dynamic inequality whose composition is driven by competence in the multiple dimensions that status is measured?"

We have that chance with Bitcoin for example. For the first time in history, the capacity to move upwards exists because those "at the bottom" can officially save and protect the product of their labor, and downward mobility exists because those "at the top" can no longer socialize their losses by printing new money, or shifting the cost of bad decisions onto those they 'represent'.

In an organic, capitalist society where the political-ruling class is unable to arbitrarily conjure money out of thin air for themselves, if you add more value, do more work, provide a better service, build a better product or make better choices in life, you will climb. If you consume more than you produce, if you are wasteful, if you make bad investment decisions, if you blow all your money on parties and alcohol, then guess what, you can't print any more or tax others to pay for your losses. You will fall down the social ladder.

That is fair, and the result is unequal.

And that's exactly as it should be.

> *"True equality is equality in probability."*
>
> - Nassim Nicholas Taleb

This then allows for the emergence of functional, useful, dynamic hierarchies of competence.

Organic Hierarchies

Pecking orders are natural phenomena, found in all simple, linear and especially complex and living systems. Hierarchies must develop because life must select. In order to do so, a method of prioritization must occur. We call this a hierarchy.

By no means do I suggest that there is "one" right way. Life is not so simplistic. We exist in a complex world where hierarchies and methods for prioritization emerge across multiple dimensions. Remember that humans are subjective, value oriented beings.

So the question is not whether hierarchies should exist or not (that's like arguing about the existence of gravity), but *"in what form are they most conducive to life?"*

What end of the life <> death spectrum should we attempt to model?

On one side, we have hierarchies by decree. These are unnatural and top down enforced. They exist by fiat and because there is little to no skin in the game for select members; they form at the expense and the exclusion of many.

On the other hand, we have those which are natural and emergent. These are best classified as hierarchies of competence, where status is a function of output and outcomes. Participants also generally have 'skin in the game', thus they are both more ergodic and dynamic.

Then, of course, we have everything in between.

If modernity has shown us anything, it's that institutions that may have initially arisen due to competence and a desire for order, but cemented themselves by fiat and thus have become monopolies, will not only begin to decay, but also have unintended consequences that may pose a greater danger to existence than the original chaos they set out to manage.

Marx himself noticed that progress, or capitalism was subject to correction, although he was oblivious to the concept of 'creative destruction'. Perhaps that was a function of being born in that period, or was part of his temperament, but we now know better.

> *"In these crises, a great part not only of the existing products, but also of the previously created productive forces, are periodically destroyed."*
>
> -Marx.

Much like small, periodic forest fires are necessary for the avoidance of large-scale, once-in-a-decade, catastrophic forest fires which can destroy the topsoil, the cycles of production naturally have corrections.

One may call them crises, but they are the market signaling overproduction. They are the small forest fires which must happen regularly in order to maintain the integrity of the larger system.

Without continual correction, without that necessary feedback loop, over or underproduction can run rampant until society collapses, or natural resources are completely depleted. We've seen this countless times in centrally planned and managed nations all around the world.

What happened to the forests in China under Mao, for example, was an environmental catastrophe of a monumental magnitude that few even know about.

We even see the expression of this truth in a context those in the software industry are familiar with. Waterfall vs. Agile development. The former is pre-planned, the latter iterative. The former is centrally managed whilst the latter is directed and adjusted at the edges (decentralized). The former makes early assumptions and ultimately misses the mark, the latter constantly adapts, corrects and evolves along the way.

This once again reflects the dynamic nature of progress. Innovation is not only correcting itself all of the time through dualistic creative destruction, but it is by definition unequally distributed.

We must get out of the way and stop trying to politically and artificially control status. Society will find its own dynamic equilibrium and form its own dynamic hierarchies, naturally, through feedback and correction, risk and reward, pleasure and pain. This will happen locally, and therefore be decentralized and occur at different rates. This is progress.

Unequal Progress > Equal Destruction

Entropy is the overwhelming force that breaks the human body down over time, cools hot water and turns all 'governments of the majority' into a downward spiraling 'tyranny of the lowest common denominator'.

Life is the progressive force that reaches and counters entropy, and it does so ***through*** each individual. It cannot be equal because its rate, force and energy vary. As a result, progress is something that occurs unevenly.

Destruction on the other hand, can be applied and enforced more evenly. It is always easier to bring someone down than it is to raise them up. It is easier to destroy than it is to build. As such, politics is always subject to entropic tendencies.

The living, breathing individual is able to counter entropy. He is able to grow, expand and evolve at different rates for different reasons, and in different dimensions. He can be simultaneously pulled toward a better future and pushed away from a lousy past.

The imaginary collective has neither a soul, nor body, nor mind and cannot counter entropy. As it grows in size, it decays in integrity, as it expands it ossifies and becomes more fragile.

Growth, progress, evolution and innovation are realms of the individual.

None are linear and along the way there will be creative destruction, winners and losers, compounding and correction, but such is the beauty of life.

Marx observes that: *"The place of manufacture was taken by the giant, Modern Industry; the place of the industrial middle class by industrial millionaires, the leaders of the whole industrial armies, the modern bourgeois."*

And once again frames it in a negative light as if this final rise by the bourgeois is the last and final state.

In fact, Marxist & Luddite thinking seem to share a similar flaw in their belief that progress has some upper bound or that some final, static class structure will emerge and unless torn down by the working class, can never be changed.

As such, they naively suggest we cease all progress, equalize everyone and distribute all resources evenly as if life and society are something that can remain static or that a person's problems are solely a function of his material possessions. This shows both an extreme lack of the understanding of the human psyche and human spirit (it will always reach) and a complete lack of faith in the capacity for humanity to rise to new heights via the experimentation and ingenuity of the individuals it is composed of.

The Marxist and Luddite aim so low, they completely miss humanity's true potential. From a place of fear and lack, they've opted to build bureaucracies to preserve (and thus erode) the capital that has been generated to date. In turn, they kill the human spirit and quell its desire to reach.

This is a sad, nihilistic and petty view of humanity that results in high time preference, careless behavior and the consistent erosion of precious capital over time.

Innovation Outcompetes Monopolies

Ask a layperson how monopolies emerge and they may blindly say "capitalism." This misconception must be dealt with and dismissed if we are to progress as a species. Monopolies can neither emerge nor remain stable naturally. They can only exist by decree.

Marx points out (contradicting his prior assertions) that:

> *"The weapons with which the bourgeoisie felled feudalism to the ground are now turned against the bourgeoisie itself."*

Funnily enough, he was right, but once again not for the reasons he thought he was.

The weapons of math, science, money and free markets hold accountable those who wield them as much as they smithe those who ignore them. This is natural law and order. This is what keeps the system stable and dynamic. This is what we want.

You might say: *"Oh yes, this is easy for you to say, but if left unchecked, the greedy capitalists, industrialists, technologists, [insert other 'ists'] will acquire all of the capital available and we will be slaves to them."*

To believe this can be the case is to misunderstand the dynamic nature of life, the core tenets of innovation, and the problem of scale, ie; the larger something gets, the less agile and adaptable it becomes.

Innovation is the symbiosis of creativity and destruction on the path toward greater efficacy and efficiency. Agility, renewal, correction and rediscovery are part of its DNA, and perfectly encapsulated in the difference between Agile and Waterfall development as described earlier, or even in guerilla warfare.

It must be clearly and simply stated that unfettered capitalism can lead neither to long term concentration, centralization *or* monopolization because the competitive nature of a free market means smaller, nimbler, more agile players wield collectively more intelligence, force, competence and capability.

To believe that mere size or seigniorage can outcompete innovation, and that one big player could amass all of the wealth, is to ignore Apple overtaking IBM, Facebook dominating MySpace, Netflix obsoleting Blockbuster, Tesla outcompeting GM, market caps of decade old technology companies eclipsing century old oil companies, and Bitcoin having grown 100 million percent against the Dollar since its inception.

> *The reality is that David always beats Goliath, even when the cards are stacked against him.*

The world today operates under cronyism, and is subject to the Cantillon Effect. Governments pass regulations protecting their corporate partners from competition while their proximity to the monetary spigot means they amass ever more wealth, at the expense of the productive members of society.

As such, the game they're really playing is ***'heads I win, tails you lose'***.

But despite that advantage, large corporate partners are ***still outcompeted*** by smaller, nimbler, newer, more agile and innovative competitors.

If we can tear down the walls of cronyism, reintroduce economic-consequence to decision making (macro and micro), and enable free, voluntary trade amongst individuals, then perhaps we can create a more dynamic world in which the most competent people can raise the quality of life for everyone.

That is the power of letting the human spirit reach for the stars.

Perhaps this will bring to bear one of what seem to be Marx's more palatable desires, ie; the rise and deliverance of the master and artisan.

The Master and the Artisan

Marx points out that:

> *"Modern Industry has converted the little workshop of the patriarchal master into the great factory of the industrial capitalist. Masses of laborers, crowded into the factory, are organized like soldiers. As privates of the industrial army they are placed under the command of a perfect hierarchy of officers and sergeants."*

And for a time, he was correct. This process of systemization and centralization occurred as humans found their way up and out of the trenches, farms and slums of feudal hierarchies.

But as was mentioned earlier, even by Marx himself, the weapons used by the bourgeoisie turn against them. On the one hand, competition commoditizes labor, but on the other, new technologies, products, services and industries emerge, and with them new dimensions and demand for talent, skill and competence begin to place upward pressure onto the aggregate price of labor.

Of course that doesn't mean *all* labor, but it holds true for most variations of labor. Initially. As this competitive progression occurs, the opportunity for the non-skilled workers to become skilled emerges, which in turn creates a shortage of non-skilled, resulting in either more competition for less workers, or it becomes the forcing function for machinery and processes of automation that obsolete the role of the unskilled altogether.

Obsolescence via automation is not a 'bad' thing, as luddites and neo-luddites alike are slow to grasp, because in the aggregate, it creates upward mobility and relegates the monotonous, mindless jobs that Marxists complain about, to machinery and automaton.

In this way, more wealth is created with less effort and manual labor. Humans can then move higher up Maslow's hierarchy not via some faux decree by committee, but through ingenuity and innovation. People once again have the space to become artists, artisans and masters. As we've seen with the technology and information revolutions, entirely new forms of capital, goods and services have emerged, from content creators to software developers to Youtube celebrities and graphic designers.

Instead of as Marx put it:

"The lower strata of the middle class—the small tradespeople, shopkeepers, and retired tradesmen generally, the handicraftsman and peasants," all sinking down into the class of some arbitrary proletariat, who cannot compete with the large capitalists, through innovation and voluntary action, we've been able ***earn our way up.***

Like the double-diamond model of design, humanity *had* to grow through a period of centralization and menial-labor-obsolescence in order to emerge from poverty.

And giving 'all benefit of the times' to Marx and the luddites who preceded him, this must have genuinely been a period of hardship like no other. But not only does the journey of a thousand miles start with one step, the initial steps are always the hardest. Putting the brakes on this process was never the answer, and it never will be. Getting out of the way is.

> *"If you're going through hell, keep going."*
>
> - Churchill

It's a necessary rite of passage for all humans to eat shit before they eat caviar. Unless you're lucky and entitled. In which case, in a free market, you'll eat caviar now and may one day eat shit.

It reminds me of the quote by Edmond Dantes, before he became The Count of Monte Cristo. When asked by his teacher "The Priest" to define economics, his shorthand response was: *"dig now, money later."*

That's the law of sowing before reaping, or simply the reality of producing before consuming. The a-priori law of nature; that humanity as a collective entity had to climb up from nothing. This journey was and will by definition be hard, dirty and have setbacks along the way, but it's necessary, and from where we stand, worth it.

Chapter 2:
The Competent Individual

What is the relationship between the individual and the collective (group)?

The individual is a member of a collective, and in fact, depending on the form of measurement used (skills, job, race, gender, political leaning, sexual orientation , etc) may simultaneously be a member of multiple collectives. In fact, at different stages of his life, he may even be a part of divergent and opposing collectives.

As such, one cannot measure an individual merely by the group he or she is in at a particular point in time, or in a particular place, but must do so by their character, behavior and values.

Thus we have real individuals that make up a diverse set of groups, but no real 'group' that a diverse set of individuals always belong to.

In other words, there is no struggle between an arbitrarily defined "bourgeois" ruling class and "proletariat" underclass. There are only diverse individuals who are sometimes at odds, sometimes aligned and always different in capacity, competence, values, desires, needs and wants.

Their struggle is with those who purport to represent them and measure them as mere numbers on a spreadsheet or appendages of the state. The class or collectivist model values individuals as clones in a group, ignoring all nuance.

We believe people should be valued as individuals, and we therefore propose a model of organization placing each individual at the center of their own affairs, with the voluntary right to periodically align themselves with other individuals that share common values or goals.

This alignment may manifest as a group, an association, an alliance or a community. These may change, they may adapt, they may evolve but they should never be coercive. And in stark contrast with Marxist doctrine, their identity should be defined from within, not from without, and any categorization of the group by inside or outsiders should be subordinate to the categorization of each independent individual.

Their own competence (in whatever dimension) is the ideal measure, and a free market is a bottom-up, organic mode of cooperation. It might be messy, but so is nature, and that's what makes it beautiful.

For this to work, we counter the Marxist summation of the Communist Manifesto with our own:

In a sentence; the ***Preservation of Private Property****.*

Now you might say: "Do you mean the large mansions of the super rich who exploit the poor?" And we would say; "it doesn't matter."

In order for a system of competence to work, the same rules must apply to all participants.

The first rule is that, "Each individual owns themselves for they, their thoughts and their mind are their primary form of private property."

The second rule is, "That which an individual creates or produces using their time, energy or the resources they've appropriated through voluntary trade (or that are yet to be claimed) may become their private property."

The third rule is that an individual must survive, and as such, their action is generally directed toward self preservation in the immediate term first, followed by the same across longer time horizons. This is time-preference in action. Now always outweighs later, but as we solve for now, we can begin to expand our perspective, lengthen our time horizon and think more about later.

The more we're freed up to think about later, the more we can delay gratification and build more current capital for future use.

In fact, what building capital (savings as a pure example) does is reduce the uncertainty of the future. It's an act of self preservation.

These core principles form the basis of civilization. In their absence we can only have regression and de-civilization.

What follows these principles is the necessity to specialize and trade. No one-individual can do everything, and a group of specialists can outcompete one generalist, master or not.

As such, the competent individual must discover a way to store and save the product of his labor for not just future use, but for trade with another, from which two new problems arise:

(1) The problem of inter-subjective value and (2) the lack of coincidence of wants.

These are both solved with the technology we call money. Whilst there have been many 'forms' of money, or goods and objects used to represent 'money' (from rocks, to shells, to stones, to gold and to paper), its metaphysical nature has never changed. It's been with us from the beginning of time, and will be there until the end, so long as diverse humans with subjective needs, wants and values want to trade their ideas or the product of their labor.

In fact, the only way for competent individuals to communicate effectively is through trade, commerce and the use of an efficient language of value (money). Thus the pursuit of 'the emancipation of mankind' should not be to control another's ability to produce, consume, trade or participate in commerce, it should be to pursue the discovery of a common language of value, like mathematics, that nobody can influence or control. Money as a set of immutable rules, living in the realm of the unchangeable and objective. We believe Bitcoin has solved this problem beyond a shadow of a doubt; but more on that later.

Notice that we've referred to the 'competent individual' throughout this chapter.

The incompetent, envious, uneducated and or perhaps desperate individual may opt for the political means of self preservation and wealth acquisition; and thus confiscate it from another.

The incompetent individual wants to do away with both emergent objective reality and individual subjective value. They prefer to replace them with some form of 'blanket objectivity' by decree that everyone must conform to, infused with moral relativity (the shadow of the subjective) and encapsulated by their own form of arbitrary rule. The incompetent individual is thus more interested in 'ruling', not 'rules'. They're interested in power by decree not authority through competence. This is of course a large part of what Marx advocated:

> *"The immediate aim of the Communists is the formation of the proletariat into a class, [to] overthrow of the bourgeois supremacy, [and the] conquest of political power by the proletariat."*

Karl Marx, The Communist Manifesto

Property

The distinguishing feature of the Individual is the ability to direct themselves as they see fit, and to choose means that lead to desired ends. Whether they achieve the ends or not is another question, and one whose answer is a complex blend of competence, timing, luck, circumstance, persistence and innumerable other factors. True success cannot be decreed.

In any case, to do this, the individual must be in control of their own property.

Private property begins with the individual, their mind, their body and their spirit. It extends to the material resources we've acquired through voluntary trade or initial acquisition, that we've chosen to blend our time, energy and efforts with.

This is where private property meets capitalism.

Remember that capitalism is merely the process of transforming chaos into something more orderly. The new order comes with a new set of unknowns (in aggregate; chaos), which necessitates transforming a higher chaos into higher order. And so the process goes.

But, according to Marx and The Communist Manifesto, we must ***abolish all private property***.

What does this even mean? Marx attempts to clarify by pointing to nine tenths not having property and thus abolition of property meaning its confiscation from the arbitrarily classified people he calls the Bourgeoisie, alongside their 'means of production'.

To this we say, who are these people? Who gets to define them? Who decides who is part of what group or what class? Where is the line of private property as defined by Marx as opposed to that which is defined by the original property owner?

Am I, because I was born to a shopkeeper now, someone who should have my individuality, independence and freedom abolished?

And if so, what does that then make me?

Your slave?

We now know, full well, the ramifications of this type of ideology. Hundreds of millions of innocent people killed at the hands of their own so-called representatives.

In abolishing private property, Communists not only give this group of representative-come-enforcers the permission to acquire, via confiscation, the property of another, but give that same group the power to determine who sits in what group.

This is an extremely dangerous framework, which as we've seen, resulted in democide after democide.

And do not dare use the age-old excuse of "this wasn't what Marx wanted", or "this wasn't real communism." The problem is not the ruler, but the flawed doctrines upon which the arbitrary rules are built.

The abolition of the individual's right to own and acquire private property as a function of their own labor, ingenuity, skill or talent not only destroys the private property itself, but the very foundation of individual freedom, and the desire, inspiration and motivation to pursue better ends.

The greatest tragedy of communism is not only the death of millions, but the death of their souls whilst still living.

There is no magical end-state in which privation is removed and all humans are equally happy. This is the belief of a fool. The human spirit reaches and the human mind solves problems.

Our highest and best is discovered when we are unshackled. When we are both free and responsible individuals.

Individual and Family

Marx makes some bizarre proclamations in The Communist Manifesto, but some of the most ridiculous are his position on family.

> *"The bourgeoisie has torn away from the family its sentimental veil, and has reduced the family relation to a mere money relation."*

A blind assertion made by someone who did not even want to associate with this 'class' of people and thus had no way to validate the claim. As far as I am aware, family ties transcend money relations to this day, otherwise things like ransoms and kidnapping wouldn't be a thing!

> *"On what foundation is the present family, the bourgeois family, based? On capital, on private gain. "*

-Karl Marx

Seriously. Who gave him this idea? What is he really projecting onto others? What validation can this man make on the relationship between families he neither knows or interacts with and most importantly despises?

The family unit, has and will always be the most important unit in a healthy and functional society. It comes before the nation, the state, the community or the tribe.

The abolition of family ties particularly in the past fifty years has led to an incredibly dangerous dependence on a nameless, faceless, incompetent and absent state who views you as just another entry on a database.

Your relationship to your family is direct, personal and real. Yes it comes with disagreements, pressure, pain, prejudice, expectations and a myriad of other problems, but to replace it with an indirect, impersonal relationship with some imaginary body of representatives is perhaps one of the saddest things to occur this century.

The family is the nucleus of the cell in the body of humanity. Without it, humanity cannot exist.

We all face struggles and we're dealt different hands as we embark on this journey of life. Family is one of the most important assets *and* rewards along this journey, and instead of being abolished, should be treasured.

Communism seems to view individuals as mechanical automatons or numbers on a spreadsheet with which empirical studies can be performed and the scientific method applied.

"If only we have enough power and money, we can make everyone happy."

In doing so, it cannot help but ignore the family. It removes the humanity from our interactions and assumes only labor exists. It's as if we are entities incapable of loving each other.
We assert that the two greatest gifts we have to give are our love and our labor, and it's only when we first own both, and are able to give them freely to whom we choose, that they are meaningful. This is why family is such a sacred institution.

Furthermore, beyond love and labor, family plays an important role in the development of an individual, their habits, their character and their intellect.

The Family serves as a source of structure, lessons and instruction for later on in life, and whilst many (if not all) are by some definition dysfunctional, the answer is not their abolition but their continual adaptation and improvement across generations.

A communist may believe the family is only good for child exploitation, cheap labor and private gain, but the individual understands that this sacred unit delivers many of the essential parts of what makes humans human.

- Structure
- Security
- Love
- Education
- Belonging
- Identity
- Fulfillment
- Support

Lastly, through cooperation and a blend of both love and labor, families can accomplish much more together than lone individuals with empty ties to a soulless state could ever hope to.

The Individual and the Sacred Union

Communists would have you believe that the arbitrarily defined 'class of bourgeois' people only view women as *"mere instruments of production."*

Once again, Marx is found projecting his view of women and relationships upon not only another person, but an entire population. He suggests that the relationship between men and women in this 'class', apparently foreign and repugnant to him, are merely incarnations of the exploitations of his labor theory of value.

As such, in his twisted mind, the solution is to just make all women 'common property' because these 'bourgeois' are using them as property anyway!

By Marx's own assertion, "*The Communists have no need to introduce community of women; it has existed almost from time immemorial.*"

I'm not sure where he and Engels sourced these ideas from, or how anybody chose to believe them, but these projections are neither factual, nor are they wholesome. They lead to versions of society in which everyone vaguely owns everyone else, and no***body*** is sacred, contrary to our natural inclinations that are the result of millions of years of evolutionary biology.

Much like the abolition of family, we reject the communist's desire to abolish the sacred union between man and woman, and turn them into mere mechanical units incapable of individual thought, expression and love.

The Individual and the Nation

> *"The Communists are further reproached with desiring to abolish countries and nationality.*
>
> *The working men have no country. We cannot take from them what they have not got. "*
>
> *The Communist Manifesto*

In this case, Marx may have been onto something. But not in the direction or for the reasons you may think.

Yes, nations are largely made up constructs, but they are in some sense emergent. Nobody specifically decreed a language or a culture or a nationality at the beginning, but they emerged through the competitive conquests of different groups throughout history.

In that sense, we all have some relationship with a land, a group of people, a culture and a lineage.

Does this mean we should be subjected forcefully to nationalities? I think not, and agree with Marx that 'country' should be abolished, but because we should unify all proletarians into one class, but because it is secondary or even tertiary to individual character and local tribe.

The individual is what matters, not their race, nationality, religion or class.

There is added complexity when it comes to boundaries, and this is where we really diverge, because we view a functional society as a patchwork of localities or cities.

This does away with 'nations' long term, but it does not do away with borders.

To have diversity, there needs to be local homogeneity. (Homogeneity does not scale).

And to have internal or local homogeneity, there must be strong borders.

Similar to cells in the body, they have a boundary. This reason is also why your house has walls, your iPhone a pin code and you have a door to your bathroom.

Boundaries and borders matter and furthermore they demarcate private property, assisting with our one-sentence assertion: **"Preservation of private property"**

A "common property utopia" is not only impractical, but entirely nonsensical. It is incompatible with basic privacy and the idea of personal space. Walking into some random house, whenever and for whatever reason you may deem necessary, doesn't work well, neither does defecating in front of others because the bathroom is a boundary-free-common-property.

If you don't believe me, try either one day and report back with your result.

So while a common ground for the communist and the individual is the recognition that," the working man has no country", the raison d'etre differs because the individual asserts that he is not and should not be owned by any particular group of people, including country and class, and can thus erect his own boundaries according to the outline of his property.

Love and Labor

Marx points out that capitalism leaves "*remaining no other nexus between man and man than naked self-interest, then callous 'cash payment'.*"

This statement has truth in it, but misses the important nuance.

Yes, the capitalist relationship between entities is one of calculation and cash payment, but one must remember what cash payment means.

To pay with cash means to trade the product of one's labor. As we've mentioned, the two most sacred things a human has to give in this life is their love and their labor, the latter being a function of their most scarce and precious, measurable/fungible resources; time & energy.

So yes, the common language and method of calculating the relative, subjective value between people is the 'cash payment' - and that's a beautiful thing.

Without it, we cannot trade. We are lost in the ever relative world of inter-subjective value and can no longer function. Marxism or communism deals with this problem by making decrees on how everything should be valued for everyone; presupposing we're all mindless, identical copies of each other who all have the same needs, wants and desires.

This is once again a bleak view of the world.

In a free world, cash payment is the common language that enables the solution to the problem of inter subjective value and furthermore, gives individuals the choice to accept more or less cash, because they may want more of the 'love' element than 'labor' in their interaction.

With loved ones, I may not care to measure my labor when I choose to give them something.

With those I don't know, I may choose to put myself first, to love myself and to charge for my labor.

This is a functional world and resembles the kinds of interactions that happen in nature.

This is something worth aspiring toward.

You might counter with the story of a Scrooge. And we would agree. There is of course always a Scrooge. A cold, calculating, nakedly self-interested individual who cares not for love, but only for the calculation of labor in all interactions.

How does a 'free market' solve for this 'problem'?

Simple. Scrooge ends up alone, un-loved and in many cases resented. There is a price to pay for all forms of behavior. The price may just not be in the form of a cash payment but in the form of intangible, immeasurable costs which communist ideology doesn't seem to believe exist.

Furthermore, because everyone's time will come to an end, the ultimate cost is financial anyway. This Scrooge may not have anyone left to pass it onto. In this case, the wealth he may have sold his humanity for will either end up being spent (ie; distributed to others and back into the world) or perhaps squandered by his kin or the vultures who never earned it. Once again, it will have been used up and distributed back out into the world.

The outcome is always the same. There is no need for distribution by decree.

Distribution can and will happen organically, and when competence is central and hard work accurately remunerated (fix the money, fix the world), wealth will flow to whoever deserves it.

A New Axis

History is a story of revolution and revelation. Of struggle and triumph, of heroes and villains and of leaders and followers across multiple dimensions.

Marxism and The Communist Manifesto would have you believe this all culminated into one final class struggle between two arbitrarily defined groups; the working class and their bourgeois overlords.

We propose that these battle lines have been incorrectly drawn, and the result is one which has eroded the human soul even in the face of staggering technological progress.

We propose that the real revolution, and the one in which the tools to finally win exist, is between the Sovereign Individual and the Collectivist State.

Individuals have been lumped into various groups which do not and cannot take into account their various and ever-changing wants, needs and desires. Their minds have been hijacked by propaganda that aims to diminish their natural gifts, dilute their worth, do away their soul and turn them into a barcode, or better yet a battery for use by the grand apparatus of the state.

To liberate the world and emancipate humanity from tyranny, the individual must become the locus of civilization.

This cannot be done by collectively organizing resources and power into the hands of yet another political group! This can only lead to more unfair exploitation, across new dimensions.

This emancipation can only occur when the individual is independent and responsible, when they are subject to both economic reward and economic consequence through voluntary participation, or lack thereof. In a word; when the Individual is Sovereign.

In order to claim it and return local power to the individual, the following measures may be applicable:

1. The absolute preservation of private property rights. For everyone, all the time.

2. The abolition of all taxation and its replacement with voluntary fee-for-service.

3. The right and responsibility to defend oneself in the preservation of life, liberty and private property.

4. The abolition of any and all Central Banks which use fiat money and credit expansion to enrich themselves at the expense of the population who uses it.

5. A movement onto a common, organic, emergent monetary standard which cannot be managed, controlled, ruled or issued by any group, organization, institution or nation.

6. The replacement of large scale nation states with a patchwork of city-states that are economically accountable and governed by local property owners with skin in the game.

7. The reintroduction, assertion and primacy of the family unit.

8. The abolition of all public schooling and state indoctrination programs, and their replacement with private, diverse forms of education delivered by family and passionate, competent teachers, mentors and masters.

9. The abolition of government intervention into business and industry, and the establishment of competitive meritocracies in which competence, skill, talent and hard work are rewarded, and not group identities.

10. The abolition of the welfare state, its replacement with voluntary, private charity, and the responsibility of each able person to provide for their own needs, as well as ownership for their own outcomes.

Chapter 3:
Capitalism's Phantom Variations

The Debauchery of Capitalism

> *"The best way to destroy the capitalist system is to debauch the currency. By a continuing process of inflation, governments can confiscate, secretly and unobserved, an important part of the wealth of their citizens. By this method they not only confiscate, but they confiscate arbitrarily; and, while the process impoverishes many, it actually enriches some.*
>
> *As the inflation proceeds and the real value of the currency fluctuates wildly from month to month, all permanent relations between debtors and creditors, which form the ultimate foundation of capitalism, become so utterly disordered as to be almost meaningless; and the process of wealth-getting degenerates into a gamble and a lottery."*

- Comrade Lenin

In George Orwell's iconic book, 1984, he introduced the reader to terms such as "NewSpeak" and "DoubleThink". These were specially designed means of controlling the thought processes of the population via limitations on vocabulary, inversion of definitions ("freedom is slavery," "war is peace") and a system of brutal surveillance. Their purpose was to prevent complex thought or the expression of any concept not in line with the totalitarian government's orthodoxy. The literal transformation of complex humans into simple database entries.

Unfortunately, instead of serving as a warning, his book seems to have been used as a template by modern governments in order to deliver us dystopian utopias.

This has not been more evident to the free thinking individual than in the past 24 months. We now have fact checkers, ministries of truth, 'health' camps, content police, mass censorship, distortion of definitions, approved speech, language hygiene and a never ending barrage of relativistic propaganda that only serves to confuse and madden everyone.

Words like capitalism and elite have completely lost their meaning and bring to mind "monopolies, exploitation and politicians", when in fact they mean something very different. The corollary is also true. When you hear progressives speak of "education" it might often mean "indoctrination" and "freedom of speech" often means "approved speech."

This is why we felt it important to start this book with a set of definitions. To get to the truth, we must work from an objective standard.

As such, let us turn our attention to a word used by Marx and often viewed as the opposing political system to communism; Capitalism.

It is our contention that Capitalism has nothing in common nor is in alignment with ***any*** form of politics. Capitalism, as discussed in the definitions at the outset, is an apolitical, organic process and it therefore exists irrespective of the political order. In totally top-down controlled territories it is known as 'the black market' or even barter between the farmer and the artisan, whilst in rather free and open territories it manifests as trade between private individuals and/or entities.

The problem is and always has been the projection of political modalities onto this organic process. So let us dispel these notions by reviewing some of the most common and separating them from both 'Capitalism' and 'free markets'.

> *"Intellectual freedom cannot exist without political freedom; political freedom cannot exist without economic freedom; a free mind and a free market are corollaries."*
>
> — Ayn Rand

Cronyism

Capitalism's most commonly associated modern political modality is Cronyism.

Often referred to as "crony-capitalism," if you ask most people today to define capitalism, they will likely list out the attributes of a Cronyist political apparatus.

Cronyism occurs when private entities use the public apparatus to change the rules and give themselves special rights or privileges. In other words, politicians and governments are incentivised to give particular businesses and industries an unfair advantage because as the 'representatives of the people' they have the monopoly right to do so.

In this environment, select companies excel and amass disproportionate wealth because they do not compete on a level playing field. Instead of succeeding by virtue of competence and innovation, at the constant risk of failure, they instead thrive through the use and exploitation of government granted regulatory moats, protectionism and bailouts, *at the constant risk of the taxpayer or holder of money issued by the state.*

This is the very definition of a 'moral hazard'.

Nothing could be further from raw, natural capitalism. If you jump off a cliff, you are likely to die, and you cannot expect the person who did **not** jump to die on your behalf. Likewise you cannot expect someone else to go to the gym and lose the weight 'for you'.

In cronyism, the poor decisions made by one group are paid for by another group who were neither privy to the decisions being made, nor asked permission to have their resources used for this purpose.

Raw capitalism involves correction, risk and creative destruction. Rewards can only come at the expense of risk, and to lower this expense, risk must be removed (ie; choosing not to jump from a cliff), not simply re-priced and borne by another without their consent.

This is why Cronyism is the political incarnation that most often gives the organic capitalist process a bad name.

The existence of a "State" with a monopoly not only on the use of violence, but the issuance of money and the power to both legislate and regulate, means that there will exist a tendency toward Cronyism and protectionism with a commensurate move away from free markets. A State monopoly shall always tilt a society toward regulation, favored terms, new legislation and the socialization of risk via the issuance of newly printed money and the subsequent devaluation of the savings of all holders of that money.

This abomination and perversion of capitalism, and its association with 'business' is why regular people conclude that the game is rigged. Their intuition is right, but what they've taken aim at is not.

We intend to correct that aim, and point their frustration to where it matters.

To do so, like Marx and Engels before us, we will give some color to the multiple variations of Cronyism that masquerade as Capitalism.

Central Banking and the Banking Cartels

The Great Financial Crisis of 2008, was precipitated by banks who created an ever increasing array of dangerous financial products using leverage. These derivatives, specifically, CDOs, or Collateralized Debt Obligations and CDSs, or Credit Default Swaps, related to mortgages and were used as ways to effectively re-price risk and hide it.

The result was initially like somebody got their hands on a money printer and just made a bunch of wealth appear out of nowhere. They were flying high like Icarus with his waxed wings. As the story goes, this fraud came to an end, the cost of the risks came to bear and the fallout almost seized up the entire, complex, interconnected global markets.

As things collapsed, the banking cartels gathered government officials (your representatives) and central bankers into a room to "solve the problem" they created. They used this proximity to enact changes to existing laws to protect their own hides and to essentially cover their losses with both tax-payer guaranteed money (government backstop) and the creation of a series of monetary policy programs which to date have only continued to bloat, accelerate and devalue the money, and therefore wealth, of anybody who is forced to trade their time and energy for this 'money'. In other words, they caused the problem, they kept the gains, and when it fell over, you paid for the losses. Moral Hazard.

In the end, nobody was held accountable, the banks restructured and a decade on they are not only richer, more powerful and more intertwined with the financial markets, but they are doing the same thing again. New derivatives, under new names with the knowledge that if things go bad, their losses will once again be socialized.

In a free market subject to raw capitalism, not only would these banks never have grown so large in the first place, but any such behavior would have ultimately resulted in failure. There would not have been a government available to acquire regulatory favors from, nor a central bank to bail them out. From their rubble, new, more sensible and responsible money managers and local banks would have emerged.

Perhaps on a long enough timescale, their fraudulent behavior may be the price humanity had to pay to discover Bitcoin.

Technocracies

A technocracy is an attempt to replace the poor decision making by central planners with algorithms and technologies that are more accurate at defining and predicting problems and thus proposing solutions.

Once again, we see the desire to replace holistic emergent thinking done by an array of diverse individuals, with some empirical, centrally enforced model that assumes humans are reducible to numbers and our actions to equations.

Faith in morality and kinship is replaced with faith in experts and the prevailing 'science' of the state. Large scale technology companies function like utilities, censorship becomes the norm, surveillance becomes ubiquitous and access becomes dependent upon social credit scores.

We need not remind anyone of this reality. One just needs to search "Mass Formation Psychosis" in google to discover the truth for themselves.

This utilitarian, sterile version of Cronyism is once again so far removed from natural, organic capitalism it's like comparing potatoes to rocket ships. The only difference between it and the banking cartel model described earlier is that central planners behind red curtains get replaced by central planners behind keyboards, while banks get replaced by the tech companies on the stock exchange.

In fact, the ultimate goal of the technocrat is for some form of artificial intelligence as government and centrally issued cryptocurrency as money, combining to encapsulate and control all life under a digital panopticon.

Once again, Bitcoin stands in the way of this bleak future. One can only hope we wake up in time.

Monopolies

One of the most common criticisms of Capitalism is, if left unchecked, power and wealth will concentrate in the hands of a few and monopolies will subsequently form. They argue, in a free-market environment, dominant companies can outcompete their competitors and once they've been abolished, the monopoly raises prices for sub standard goods and services.

We dispelled this notion earlier in the manifesto when we established the superiority of innovation over size.

Monopolies cannot exist in an environment of unfettered competition. If they could, the unfettered competition of the natural world would have left us with but ONE species on each continent. Every other one would have been eaten.

This is not how complex systems with diverse entities and unique individuals operate. They are interdependent, and the process of creative destruction will bring with it new dimensions of competition, progress and growth along with which come new opportunities.

What seem like monopolies may last for a period, and in fact, with access to the ultimate monopoly (the state) they can extend their shelf life through regulatory moats, protectionism and proximity to the monetary spigot - we see this today with banks, pharmaceuticals, energy companies and the like. The barriers to entry are so high that innovation is stifled - but in the end, even they succumb to the overwhelming force of innovation and progress.

Amazon, whilst having created immense prosperity in its wake, is now a good example of this. It started off as an innovative company which outcompeted in the marketplace, but over time evolved into a behemoth thanks to easy money policies created by the central bank, overheated stock market valuations and preferential credit markets that allowed Amazon to run at a loss for decades while gobbling up small retailers around the world, who were unable to keep the doors open without producing a profit.

Furthermore, ridiculous government lockdowns and mandates alongside favorable regulations made it one of the only businesses able to thrive during one of the most difficult economic periods in recent history. All of this is a function of an upstream monopoly who can shift the cost of their poor decision making onto a populace, without consent.

This is the leviathan we're fighting, and not with a new political power, but with innovation, private property, responsibility and free trade. Combined, these virtues of liberty cannot be beaten because once in a while, something so groundbreaking enters the fray, that no amount of protectionism or regulatory advantage can save them.

We believe Bitcoin is that kind of 'zero to one' moment, not just for money, but for the organization of society at large. This is not only a disruption to banking and payments, but ***the*** disruption of the central planning, central banking, nation state model of the world.

Oligopolies

Oligopolies are an extension of Monopolies, and are merely cartels that exist to give the illusion of competition. They are no different to any of the above and function just like appendages of the state, only with multiple heads.

They come in all forms, including banking cartels, chemical cartels, big pharma and large scale technology firms.

We need not belabor this point further, except to state clearly that it is neither a form of Capitalism, nor synonymous with free markets in which competition is king.

Political Capitalism

A complete misnomer, and something which cannot exist.

In order to move toward a world in which individuals can be in charge of their destiny, we must separate politics from economics, alongside separating state from money.

Conservatism / The Right

Many people today believe that conservatives, or Republicans or 'the right' are somehow representatives of Capitalism.

The truth is that the organic capitalism process needs some bureaucrats to represent it about as much as the ocean needs you to jump in there and form waves with your hands.

The Republicans are the original gangsters when it comes to Cronyism. They wrote the manual. It was the liberals who later took things to another level.

Capitalism is not a political philosophy, nor a right or left wing ideology.

It is a natural process all human beings undertake as they transform chaos into order.

Conservatives, not necessarily the same as right wing politicians, generally err toward recognizing long-standing, lindy-compatible heuristics as ways to organize society. As such, they tend to get out of the way of the capitalist process more-so than progressives who believe that we need to manage everything.

Republicans, not necessarily conservative, believe politics comes before economics and as such use their position to gain advantage, often at the expense of those they purport to represent.

As you will note, we propose an entirely new axis and a move toward the abolition of mass representation at scale, in favor of local decision making and freedom.

Democracy

Instead of being represented as the parasite which has benefited from the prosperity of free markets and continues to leech resources, capital, capacity and energy alongside it, democracy is thought of as the 'source' of prosperity and free markets.

This couldn't be further from the truth. First and foremost, voluntary exchange existed long before this method of rule, and will do so long after it is gone. Secondly and more importantly, the under-current for all progress is productivity, innovation and exchange, NOT political rule.

Humanity has evolved ***despite*** its political chains, not thanks to them.

The source of human flourishing and progress has and always will be the free and voluntary exchange of private individuals who respect each other's private property rights and tap into their individual ingenuity to be ever more useful and productive.

The fact that it has been conflated with dEmOcRaTiC rule is one of the greatest fallacies of modern society.

For Greeks writing in the ancient Athenian city state, democracy was simply mob rule. It was the politics of the crowd. Demagogues would use rank flattery of base passions and fears to move public opinion whichever way they wished.

Plato held that a pure democracy is always one step away from devolving into tyranny, because a sufficiently accomplished manipulator of the crowd can rise to power on waves of popular adulation and then turn himself into a tyrant.

Democracy is an affront to capitalism, because nature does not recognize politics, and the only vote that matters is where one chooses to spend and deploy the product of their labor. In other words, you vote with your feet and your money.

Attempting to obfuscate that process and place a series of decision layers in between such that a representative can make unhinged economic decisions on the behalf of everyone that both wanted and did not want to be represented is not only reprehensible, but inefficient and ineffective. Thus directly counter to the forcing functions of capitalism!

Democracy is the most dangerous when combined with any version of cronyism as the unproductive majority will always wish to vote themselves more benefits paid for by the more productive minority. Hence modernity.

Colonialism

Colonialism is a practice or policy of control by one people or power over another territory, often by establishing colonies and generally with the aim of economic dominance. Many people have been taught that capitalism leads to colonialism, and so believe they are one in the same, but if we examine both at their most basic level, you can see this is not the case.

The central characteristics of capitalism include competitive markets, private property rights, voluntary exchange, innovation and trade.

Colonialism is a practice of domination, which involves the subjugation of one people to another, and cares less about trade, and more about force, imposition and oftentimes, confiscation.

Capitalism respects private property, Colonialism takes it away.

Capitalism requires voluntary exchange, Colonialism subjugates one people to another.

Conflating the two does nobody a service and only places people on the path toward either revenge or throwing the baby out with the bathwater.

Capitalism: A New Axis

Each of the aforementioned versions of non-capitalism are merely forms of collectivism. In fact, part of why we wrote this is to assist you, the reader, in re-adjusting your own axis.

Capitalism is neither right nor left. It has nothing to do with politics.

As we have noted, Capitalism is a mode of organic "being". All living species by definition evolve and grow by taking scarce resources, time and energy (capital) and transforming them into something of high order virility or value.

The spectrum of humanity is therefore not "left and right" politics, but capitalism on one end, and politics on the other, with the political end having a spectrum of its own. The graph actually looks more like a T, and each end has its own veritable characteristics.

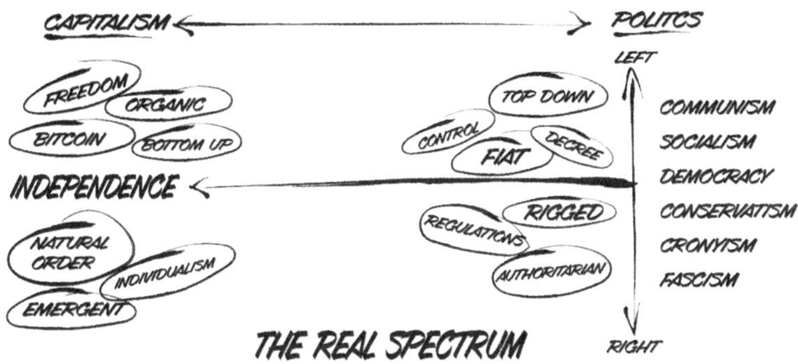

Centralization of control and decision making is characteristic of the political end. Politics in whichever flavor, is the making of decisions by representatives and the subsequent distribution of the represented's resources or status. In this type of system, political players use non-productive, coercive means to build status and wealth for themselves.

Capitalism is decentralized. It occurs at the edge, as a function of voluntary participation by the individual, in a free market. It is bottom up, emergent and requires work, intelligence, competence and ingenuity in order to progress.

As such, capitalism forms dynamic hierarchies around competence. Control is distributed, dominance revolves and quality spirals upward by virtue of competition.

In contrast, political hierarchy and authority are simply a function of decree, and as a result they always decay. Despite the attempts by Socialists, Communists or other utopian idealists to remove hierarchies, often by force, they inevitably fail to do so. Something new fills the vacuum, and it is always a new hierarchy, because humans must prioritize and organize.

Since hierarchies will always form, either by virtue of competence if allowed to emerge in the free market, or by violence and the artificial decree of popularity contest winners in the game of "politics" (and the vacuum of competence), we must think deeply about which kind we want.

Austrian Economics

Of all the studies of economics, the most aligned with the natural process of Capitalism is the Austrian school of economics, whose founding fathers include the likes of Carl Menger, Ludwig Von Mises, Friedrich Hayek & Murray Rothbard.

Austrian economics does not seek to model, predict or organize an economy but rather to understand axiomatic, a-priori truths and then infer how the most complex of systems, the economy of human beings, may respond to certain stimuli. It is interested in studying praxeology, better known as 'human action', the marginal and subjective theories of value, human behavior and incentives.

It recognizes that you cannot build models that represent the real world, because you cannot rewind time, nor can you replicate the actions of all individuals from one moment to the next. It acknowledges that all individuals differ in their wants, needs, goals and desires, instead of attempting to fit multi-dimensional humans into empirical models or spreadsheets.

Austrian Economics stands in direct opposition to modern, Keynesian and neoclassical economics. It opts to consider and analyze "practical actions" as a way to understand the market, rather than statistics and models.

Austrians emphasize private property, entrepreneurship, free markets, and sound money as the key drivers of economic performance, and the subjective values and actions of real actors as the ultimate cause of all economic outcomes.

Austrians also believe that markets should be free from "government interference" and that attempted government control of a market can only lead to distortions. Markets are not a machine that can be built and managed, instead they are living organic complex systems that self regulate if left to run of their own accord.

We encourage you to dig further into this school of thought.

Free Markets

If Austrian economics is the study of capitalism, a free market is its manifestation.

A market, free from government intervention and centrally enforced control, regulations, taxes, tarifs and licenses is a market which can thrive and find its own equilibrium. Its forcing functions are supply, demand, production and need, and its operation is decentralized and localized.

In a free market, companies and resources are owned by private individuals or entities who are free to engage, contract and trade with one another. Yes, there may be bad actors, but in a free market, reputation becomes paramount and over time, bad economic actors fare poorly. Furthermore, skin in the game ensures cost is localized and moral hazard reduced. You will treat your own car far better than you will treat a rental car.

There are few truly free markets in the world today, only markets that operate on the spectrum from controlled to somewhat free. The names given to truly free markets are the gray and black markets which emerge from beneath government suppression, and they manifest, for example, as the life-saving supplies into North Korea, East Germany, Soviet Russia, War Camps, Prison Camps and countless other downstream consequences of the actions of state monopolies.

Bitcoin

Bitcoin is the most powerful, organic incarnation of capitalism that has emerged in the modern world. It is an apolitical money whose rules are the same for everyone, are fixed, auditable, verifiable and voluntary to opt into.

It is a money with no leader, and through proof of work has managed to successfully merge the metaphysical nature of money to the physical laws of the universe. As such, for the first time in human history we have perfect, fixed, immutable money that bridges the gap between the physical and digital, tying bits to atoms and giving us the best of both worlds.

Being a borderless, permissionless network that is open and free, any individual can own and control property developed, built on, or connected to the network. And because it cannot be coopted or controlled, it results in the purest form of private property, with the lowest cost of defense and highest cost to attack. This change in the returns to violence incentivises cooperation over theft and results in a transformation of the relationship between the would-be 'governors' and the 'governed' from subject-overlord, into customer-service provider.

No other technological-social-economic-physics phenomenon exists or has existed with the potential to truly break the monopoly power of the collectivist state and move the locus of control of each individual back into their own hands.

It is the ultimate tool of The Sovereign Individual, and with it we're hopeful there is finally a way to transcend politics and swing back to the organic, Capitalist end of the spectrum.

Capitalism; The Economic System

Whilst it is true that capitalism, the organic process, both transcends and permeates all systems of coordination (whether left, right, conservative or progressive), and merely defines the progressive process all human beings undertake, one can observe characteristics emerge in its application and possibly derive methods of better understanding it and enabling its continuation.

Austrian Economics helps us understand.

Free markets are how we operate.

Bitcoin is what makes it all possible.

With these ingredients, we may derive a new, 'Local Capitalism' as an economic system.

One in which private property rights are central, where individuals (or groups of individuals) control the means of production and measure their operation in the production of excess value (profit). Where all decision-making for property and capital is determined by the private owners of said property and capital.

Core characteristics of this model may include, but not be limited to capital accumulation, competitive markets, a price system determined by supply and demand, defensible preservation of private property rights, free and voluntary trade, private judicial bodies, competitive insurance, fee for service protection and voluntary participation in local decision making.

By economically empowering the individual, they are free to choose and be responsible for their lifestyle, personal relationships and associations, and one's own artistic, moral, esthetic and cultural choices.

This is our path to a better, more just, diverse, wealthy, rational, functional and free world.

Instead of building a long tail of lemmings with captured minds, we can build a group of productive, sovereign individuals with free minds.

> *"a free market is a corollary of a free mind".*
>
> *Ayn Rand*

The Matrix:

CHARACTERISTICS	CAPITALISM	CRONYISM	CONSERVATISM	COLONIALISM	COMMUNISM	FASCISM
Private Ownership	Y	N	Y	N	N	N
Private Control of Production	Y	P	Y	N	N	N
Private Property Rights	Y	P	Y	N	N	N
Free Markets	Y	P	S	N	N	N
Capital Accumulation	Y	Y	Y	P	N	P
Competitive Markets	Y	P	P	P	N	N
Market Pricing	Y	P	P	P	N	P
Voluntary Exchange	Y	P	P	N	N	N
Voluntary Participation	Y	P	P	N	N	N
Emergent, Common Language of Value	Y	N	N	N	N	N
Risk & Consequence At All Layers	Y	N	N	N	N	N
Large Scale Government	N	Y	Y	Y	Y	Y
State Controlled Means of Production	N	P	P	P	Y	P
Central Banking	N	Y	Y	Y	Y	Y

Yes, we realize this chart is on its side, and turning the book sideways is hard, but we kept it this way so you could actually read the text. You're welcome.

PS. You can download all the charts free here: *UnCommunist.com/charts*

Chapter 4:

Position of the Individual in Relation to the State

The true struggle is therefore the battle between individual autonomy and collectivist coercion.

One of human nature VS artificial control. Not of one group against another.

Marxists, in their bid to impose an arbitrary identity on groups of individuals, actually created, by decree, two new groups:

1. The 'public representatives', who on 'behalf' of the people hold all of the power.

2. The 'private individual', who is commonly owned, has none of the power, cannot stand alone and is forcefully represented by some empowered via a vague 'will of people'.

The latter form a sort of modern slave, transformed from diverse humans into a homogenous blob of mindless masses. The proof is all around you.

The former, the "representatives" amass all of the power. Those who are best at making the most promises, confiscating and redistributing the most wealth and convincing as many people as possible that "they care" rise to the top. All the while, 'open access' to the political system gives everyone the illusion of choice.

We end up with complete and absolute rule by the imaginary, arbitrary "collective", represented by the most adept politicians and power brokers, instead of a dynamic fragmented, local order of the competitive and competent Individual.

Human Nature

Human nature is boundless. It will forever evolve and adapt. Making it static is the true death.

> *"Of all the classes that stand face to face with the bourgeoisie today, the proletariat alone is a really revolutionary class. The other classes decay and finally disappear in the face of Modern Industry; the proletariat is its special and essential product."*
>
> -Marx

Marx seems to have lacked any understanding of either human psychology or the dynamic nature of groups.

People will always gather and organize themselves across innumerable dimensions. To claim that one final class of workers is the be-all and end-all for society assumes that progress will cease, that diversity will give way to homogeneity, that we are all somehow the same, and that we will all conform to the desires of a single group identity.

Humans are not looking to just be 'fed and asleep'. We are so much more complex.

As Dr. Peterson so beautifully states; in many ways, we're looking to keep looking.

The pursuit of material ends and an equally distributed material utopia is such a shallow conception of the way the human mind and spirit work.

We go out looking for problems. We transform chaos into order. We struggle and forge ourselves into higher beings, and better versions of ourselves.

The attempted removal of privation does not solve all of humanity's problems! The aspects and scope of the struggle will merely transform.

And in fact it has. The seeds of the struggle to retain autonomy as an individual have today transformed into the struggle to become and remain a Sovereign Individual, wresting independence from the clutches of the collective.

The struggle has and always will be multidimensional, but at its core, it is to first thrive and then become the best version of yourself.

Why is Marxism so Appealing?

It is easier to bring someone down than it is to raise them up. It is easier to destroy than it is to build. The tendency toward entropy is the overwhelming force that turns all 'governments of the majority' into a downward spiraling tyranny of the lowest common denominator.

Marxism gives some people a convoluted academic justification for envy, resentment, laziness and a sense of entitlement; all forms of behavioral entropy.

Nevermind that the Communist Manifesto is full of contradictions, hyperbole, blanket assumptions about people they neither knew nor liked and the arbitrary classification of people into two classes to be pitted against each other.

Some people merely wanted to justify their sloth, their envy and their malice.

I quote:

> *"They direct their attacks not against the bourgeois conditions of production, but against the instruments of production themselves; they destroy imported wares that compete with their labor, they."*

Translated into simple english, he says; *"if you cannot outcompete them, burn it all down."*

Are these not the words of a mindless animal? This quote sums up the morality of Marx and the basis upon which all collectivist ideologies stand.

> *"If you can't make something better, burn it all down."*

Or more succinctly (and unfortunately historically accurate):

> *"If you can't beat them, kill them."*

Like their Luddite predecessors, Marx and his ilk had such little faith in human ingenuity and a low opinion of the capacity for individual improvement that instead of encouraging the proletariat to rise up to a new standard, they should bring everything down to theirs.

As I said earlier, it's easier to destroy than it is to create. It's easier to kill than it is to give life. It's easier to bring another down than it is to raise them up. The siren call of entropy is strong.

This ideology is unfortunately the product of a person who succumbed to their own inadequacies, projected it on others and in a fearful rage demanded that others remain in the dungeon of nihilism with him because he feared to be left alone.

He feared to stand up, so he wanted to cut everyone else down.

A Better Future

This is why you, dear reader, must now stand up.

You may have already found Marxism and collectivism abhorrent. Or perhaps you had succumbed to its siren call, tugging on the lower emotions we all carry within us. Perhaps you wanted to believe you could sow without reaping, or that somebody else would produce while you just consume, or that some magical force of 'the state' would always be there to provide for you, without you having to work or make sacrifices.

Perhaps you believed in equality, without enquiring any deeper into the possible ramifications of such a doctrine and its obliteration of not only diversity amongst human beings, but of the very soul crushing impact it has on them.

It's ok. We've all been wrong, we've all felt sorry for ourselves and we've all at times expected someone else to fix it for us. But there also comes a time when we must all stand up for ourselves, and once again claim a level of independence and responsibility that makes us free, unique, diverse, multidimensional individuals.

We must harness our unique gifts and talents, we must continue to develop our skills, we must align with nature, we must apply the emergent principles we've observed and inferred using apriori thinking, we must continue to economize, to trade, to compete, to strive and to grow, all so that humanity can flourish.

The collectivists openly declare that their ends may only be attained at ***your*** expense and the forcible confiscation of ***your*** property and independence. Competent individuals declare that their ends may only be attained at the expense of their own capital, effort and energy, in combination and voluntary cooperation with other competent, independent individuals.

Let the fraudulent fiat collectivists tremble at the Rise of the Sovereign Individual.

In accordance with natural order, whilst we may have something to lose (risk), we also have a better future to gain (reward).

Sovereign Individuals of the world

Stand Up and claim your Autonomy!

Afterword

Quotes and comments from some of the great minds and most sovereign individuals of the modern era.

Robert Breedlove:

"Tyrants across history have established their positions by making moral appeals on behalf of fictionalized collectives such as "the greater good," "this great nation," or "our democracy." These appeals to fictitious entities always come at the expense of real individuals—who pay in freedom, money, and blood—to fulfill the various tyrannical visions conjured up in the name of statism. In reality, only individuals can choose, prosper, and suffer—all appeals to arbitrarily circumscribed collectives are inevitably espoused by individuals pursuing their own ends. In the case of statism, these ends involve the denial of the most fundamental reality in the sphere of human action—individual self-ownership. In "The UnCommunist Manifesto," the authors thoroughly dismantle the deceptive strategies of statism to reveal the only proper path toward widespread human flourishing—absolute individual freedom, subject only to the limiting principle of private property."

George Gammon:

"Marxism or central planning is very similar to Eugenics in the sense those who believe in it, by definition, also believe there are some in society who are superior and some who are inferior. In the US we've seen that lead to legalizing forced sterilization, in other countries such as Russia and China far worse. Literally, millions of people were murdered. That's where giving a few the power, control, authority over many leads, regardless of whether it's called Marxism or Eugenics. Free market capitalism is the opposite, it's DE centralized, therefore one would expect the results from this approach to be just as amazing as central planning (Marxism/Eugenics is horrific).

And if you study places that have employed Free Market Capitalism you see this to be true."

Spike Cohen:

"Aleks Svetski and Mark Moss flip Marx and Engels on their heads. In UnCommunist Manifesto, their case is very plainly made, using both a philosophical perspective and real-world historical examples, that the real struggle is not between arbitrarily defined classes of 'oppressor' and 'oppressed', but rather the struggle of sovereign individuals to claim their autonomy. Anyone who wishes to rebut the popular narratives against capitalism and property rights would do well to read this book."

About the Authors

Aleksandar Svetski

A long time entrepreneur and writer, Aleks has founded numerous companies across a multitude of industries, his most recent being the Bitcoin finance app; Amber, and The Bitcoin Times publication.

He's most well known for his early philosophically-oriented essays on Bitcoin, and especially his more controversial takes on Democracy, 'The State' and the idea of "The Remnant".

He now spends most of his time writing, speaking, podcasting and thinking about ways in which the nature of the world will evolve as the grand cycle we're currently in comes to a close, and a new one emerges.

Find more of Aleksandar's work at: *www.svet.ski*

Mark Moss

Mark Moss is no stranger to making money—by the time he was 30, he had amassed $25 million in real estate holdings. When the housing market crashed in 2008, he lost everything. But he dusted off and rebuilt his businesses and investments, and this time, he knew that simply accumulating wealth wasn't enough. He needed to learn how to protect his wealth and gain his own financial and personal sovereignty.

Now it is his mission is to share that wisdom with as many people as possible. Through his YouTube videos with 20 million+ views, a nationally syndicated iHeart radio show, and through his online programs, Mark is helping people understand the most important issues facing the world today and what they can do to build, grow and protect their wealth.

Visit Mark's website at: *1markmoss.com*

Bonus Material

Did you enjoy the book?

Do you feel as if this message needs to be spread out further?

To learn more about how we can collectively ensure the poison that is Communism spreads no further, join us at:

UnCommunist.com/Member

The members area contains a whole host of resources which you can access at any time to further your education and to further the mission.

We've also put together a couple easy-to-access resources:

1. Charts

If you'd like to use or reference the charts in this book, you can download them for free in the members area, or via the link below:

UnCommunist.com/Charts

2. Talking Points

Many have been confronted with the nice-sounding communist ideas by both well, and not-so-well-meaning people, and because there is so much noise and confusion, it's not easy to rebut these ideas.

We've taken the time to put together a series of rebuttals to Marxist ideology that you can access for free. Whether you need to deal with a well-meaning friend, or some troll online (not that you should waste time with this, but hey...sometimes it helps), having a cheat sheet on hand may be useful. You can download them for free in the members area, or via the link below:

UnCommunist.com/CheatSheet

Member **Charts** **Cheat Sheet**

Made in the USA
Coppell, TX
26 September 2022